P9-DBR-941

feeling SAFE feeling STRONG

feeling  SAFE

feeling STRONG

How to Avoid Sexual Abuse
and
What to Do If It Happens to You

Susan Neiburg Terkel & Janice E. Rench

Lerner Publications Company · Minneapolis

J 362.7044
TERKEL

The authors would like to acknowledge the following people, whose advice and input was appreciated: Dr. Stephen Ludwig, Karen Rubin, Shirley Bonnem, The Cleveland Rape Crisis Center, Hudson Village Police, Cleveland City Police, Dr. Lora Lee Marsh, Susan Titus, our husbands, Larry Terkel and Larry Rench, and most of all, our editor, Susan Stan, for her unwavering support and ceaseless attention to detail.

Design by David Barnard
Illustrations by Rick Hanson

LIBRARY OF CONGRESS CATALOGING IN PUBLICATION DATA

Terkel, Susan Neiburg.
  Feeling safe, feeling strong.

  Summary: Fictional vignettes depict acts of child sexual abuse, such as pornography, incest, rape, and obscene phone calls; and information on handling such situations is offered.
    1. Child molesting—Case studies—Juvenile literature.
  2. Child molesting—Prevention—Juvenile literature.
  [1. Child molesting. 2. Sex crimes] I. Rench, Janice E.
  II. Title.
  HQ71.T47 1984   362.7'044   84-9664
  ISBN 0-8225-0021-3 (lib. bdg.)

Copyright © 1984 by Lerner Publications Company

All rights reserved. International copyright secured. No part of this book may be reproduced in any form whatsoever without permission in writing from the publisher except for the inclusion of brief quotations in an acknowledged review.

Manufactured in the United States of America

International Standard Book Number: 0-8225-0021-3
Library of Congress Catalog Card Number: 84-9664

  2   3   4   5   6   7   8   9   10   93   92   91   90   89   88   87   86   85

C H B

In memory of James Coughlin

—S.T.

To John, Elizabeth Ann, and Thomas Kohler

—J.R.

Contents

Feeling Safe

Wherever you are—at home, at school, or outside—you want to feel safe. And most of the time, you *are* safe.

But sometimes unexpected things happen. You might be in a shopping mall when someone you don't know begins to talk to you. It gives you a funny feeling, but you don't know why. Or you might be at home with a babysitter who wants to touch you in a place you don't want to be touched.

You have probably already learned several rules to follow to stay safe. But other situations may come up that you don't know how to handle. You might just feel uneasy, or you might feel afraid. Some of these situations *could* turn into sexual abuse.

What is sexual abuse? When an adult or older teenager forces, threatens, or bribes you into any kind of sexual contact, it is called sexual abuse.

The stories in this book tell about different kinds of touching and sexual abuse. Some of these things may have happened to you or to someone you know.

This book will help you understand the difference between healthy touching and sexual abuse. It will also give you the information you need to avoid dangerous situations.

Ashley's Story

Can't Make Me

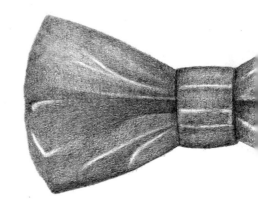

"Hurry up, we're going to be late," Mom yelled, walking past my bedroom. "If you'd put your clothes away when you take them off, you'd know where to find them when you need them. Why must you always do this to me?"

I don't know how stuffing my clothes under the bed until I need them is doing anything *to* my mother. "Mom, I'll put them away when we get back," I said. "Okay?"

When I grow up, my bedroom isn't going to have any furniture in it. Just a sleeping bag that doesn't have to be made and two areas marked off on the floor, one for dirty clothes and one for clean clothes. Only *really* dirty clothes should go in the dirty pile. Mom makes me throw stuff in the wash after I've worn it only once. Can you imagine that?

"Ashley Elizabeth Morgenstern," Mom said in *the voice,* "you are not wearing that sweatsuit to Aunt Sally and Uncle Bernie's!"

"Why not?" I asked.

"Because you look like a ragamuffin. Go to your room and put on your lavender and white dress, right now, Ashley. And," she added, as I was on my way back to my room, "if you don't comb your hair and brush your teeth and look like a decent human being, you will be punished when we get back."

"Yes, Mom," I said, not bothering to turn around. I was already being punished by going to Aunt Sally's.

I hate my lavender and white dress. The seams around the sleeves and the waist are scratchy, and all the lace on the skirt looks silly. The shoes are the worst part. They're white leather with a little bow on the top. My feet are so squashed in them that it feels like someone is stepping on my toes.

"Did you comb your hair and brush your teeth yet?" Mom asked. She acts like I need to be reminded a million times. Most of the time, I do remember. I just don't like doing it *the minute* I'm told.

Mom's all right when she isn't picking on me. In the summer we go to the beach and I roll in the sand and get as dirty as I want. She also lets me sleep late on Saturday mornings. My friend Heidi has to get up early to clean her room.

"I'm ready," I said. "Do I look all right *now?*" Of course I knew I'd be safer not saying anything or maybe saying something nice like "Gee, Mom, you look great in that outfit," but I *couldn't.* I wasn't in the mood to be nice. My dress was itchy, my feet hurt, and the last place I wanted to be on a sunny day—in fact, any day—was in Aunt Sally and Uncle Bernie's apartment.

Part of the reason is Uncle Bernie. He smells of garlic, his beard is scratchy, and he picks his teeth with a toothpick. I hate kissing him or having him kiss me. I'm afraid he'll forget about the toothpick—it's always in the side of his mouth—and stab my cheek. I hate the feel of his scratchy whiskers. Even if I just had to hug him, the smell of garlic would make me sick.

Before I got in the car, I snuck in the kitchen, stuffed some cookies in my mouth, and washed them down with milk. There was no telling what would be for dinner. Aunt Sally is always taking gourmet cooking classes. I think "gourmet" means trying to cook things most people wouldn't think of eating. The last time I ate there, Aunt Sally served squid with all the legs on and the eyes staring straight up at me.

"Mom, this food is definitely *not* for people," I whispered to her.

Mom glared at me and I got the hint to be quiet. But

then, when no one was looking, she took my squid onto her own plate and ate it.

"I can't believe it," Aunt Sally said, "Ashley cleaned her plate for a change!" Mom and I looked at each other and smiled at our little secret.

When we got in the car, I said, "What do you think Aunt Sally made for dinner? Think it's anything I'll recognize?"

"Ashley, whatever she serves you," Mom said, "I expect you to taste it without a fuss and without a face. And don't forget to chew with your mouth shut, and put your napkin on your lap."

For the next half hour I didn't say much. Mom listened to the radio and sang along to all the tunes. She's no rock star, but I give her credit for trying to sing. With her voice, it takes a lot of guts to sing even when no one's listening.

I kept thinking about how much I didn't want to go, and about all the other stuff I could be doing instead. Why, I'd rather clean my room all afternoon than go to Aunt Sally and Uncle Bernie's. The more I thought about it, the angrier I got. By the time we got to their parking lot and I saw their apartment building, I was determined not to kiss Uncle Bernie.

"Mom," I said, while we waited for the elevator, "you can make me taste disgusting food, wear awful clothes, and chew with my mouth shut, but you *can't* make me kiss Uncle Bernie!"

"Ashley, you wouldn't want to hurt Uncle Bernie's feelings," said Mom.

"What about *my* feelings?" I asked. "I *hate* to smell him, his beard scratches me, and I'm afraid he'll stab me in the cheek with his toothpick!"

"Honey, I'm sorry," Mom said, stepping into the elevator, "I had no idea he bothered you that much. Why don't you shake his hand instead? Before he realizes you didn't kiss him, I'll kiss him hello." I was as surprised and relieved as I was the time that Mom ate my squid.

"By the way, Mom," I said, as we walked down the hallway to their apartment, "you look nice today."

Facts about Personal Rights

It was Ashley's right not to kiss Uncle Bernie when she didn't feel like it. Everyone has the right to choose who to hug, kiss, and touch. Ashley's mother recognized how uncomfortable Ashley felt and helped her find another way to greet Uncle Bernie. The following information will help you learn what personal rights you have and how to stand up for them.

What are personal rights?

Every person, child or adult, is entitled to the same personal rights. "Personal" describes those things having to do with you as an individual—your body and your feelings. Your body belongs to you, not to someone else, and you have the right to keep it private if you want to. You also have the right to any feelings that you have.

How can you defend your personal rights?

Before you can stand up for your personal rights, you must first recognize how you feel. You may be happy, sad, afraid, excited, or confused. No two people feel exactly alike in the same situation. Your feelings are part of what makes you a special person.

Next, you must learn to express your feelings. You have the right to let someone know if he or she says or does anything that makes you feel uncomfortable. The first thing to do when you feel uncomfortable is to say to yourself, "I don't like this." You should then *act* on that feeling. You can say, "No, please don't do that" or "Stop, I don't like that!" Then move away, or, if you need to, run away.

It is always okay to defend your feelings, your privacy, and your safety. Never be afraid to let others know how you feel. Talk to your parents about ways of avoiding situations and people that make you feel uncomfortable. If your parents don't understand your feelings, talk them over with someone else. Maybe a close relative or friend can help.

Garth's Story

Easy Money

It was all Mr. Stanski's idea. Mr. Stanski is my neighbor, or rather *was* my neighbor. At first it sounded too good to be true. Mr. Stanski offered to pay me to model for him. All I had to do was hang around while he took pictures of me. He made me promise, though, to keep it a secret. I wouldn't have told anyone anyway, since I didn't want anyone else to horn in on a good deal.

Dirt-bike racing was starting in less than a month and I needed money for a new dirt bike. My Christmas money was long gone. I had asked Dad if he would buy me a new dirt bike.

"Garth, what's wrong with the ten-speed I just bought you last year?" he asked.

"I can't race a ten-speed on a motocross track," I said.

"When I was your age I didn't need such expensive toys, Garth. In fact, I wouldn't have had the *nerve* to ask my parents for them," he said, rubbing his chin like he

does when he's annoyed. When Dad starts talking about how things were in his day, I know that's the end of the discussion.

If I wanted a new bike, I'd just have to get the money on my own. I decided to ask my mother to pay me to do chores around the house.

"Absolutely not, Garth. Family members should never get paid for contributing to the household," she said. "Parents don't get paid for raising children, so why should children get paid for helping parents?"

Ever since Mom started going to law school last year, she challenges everything I say.

It was too early in the year to mow lawns and too late to shovel snow. So I went around the neighborhood looking for odd jobs to do. I thought maybe I could find a fence to paint like Huck Finn did.

The only fence I found was around Mr. Stanski's swimming pool, and I decided to ask him if it needed painting. Mr. Stanski is home a lot and isn't married. In the summer he has parties at his pool. I walked over to his house and rang the doorbell.

"I'm looking for odd jobs, Mr. Stanski. Could I paint your fence?" I asked when he came to the door.

"It's nice of you to offer, but the fence doesn't need painting," he answered.

I guess I looked disappointed, because after thinking for a minute, Mr. Stanski said, "I *do* have a way for you to earn some money, Garth, but it has to be a secret between you and me. Understand?"

"Sure. Just tell me what to do," I said, glad to have any job.

"I need a model for some photographs. I'll pay you twenty dollars to pose for me."

Twenty dollars! I couldn't believe my good luck. "When should I start?" I asked.

"Let's have a photography session tomorrow afternoon," said Mr. Stanski.

I thought for a second. Mom would be at school then, so I wouldn't have to tell her where I was going when I left the house. "That's perfect," I said.

The next day after school I rushed home to change my clothes and comb my hair before I went next door. When I got to Mr. Stanski's, he smiled at me. "You look great, Garth," he said. "Now remember, this job is a secret—you didn't tell anyone you were coming here, did you?"

I shook my head no. "Good, then let's get started. We'll work in the basement," he said as he began walking. "You'll look good against the fireplace."

I followed him downstairs. When I saw all the photography equipment in his rec room, including spotlights, I realized that Mr. Stanski was a professional photographer.

I sat cross-legged in front of the fireplace, elbows on my knees. I felt a little funny, since I didn't know how professional models were supposed to act.

"We're going to pretend it's the middle of summer, Garth, so I want you to take off your shirt," Mr. Stanski said. He was standing behind the camera, peering through the lens and fiddling with some knobs. It was kind of cold in the basement but I took off my shirt and tried to pretend I could feel the sun. It was hard to imagine summer standing next to the fireplace.

Mr. Stanski looked pleased, though, and took a few pictures. Every once in a while he asked me to move this way or that. Then he leaned out from behind the camera and told me take off the rest of my clothes. I must have just sat there, because he had to tell me again.

"Now take off your jeans, Garth, and your under-wear."

I took them off like he told me, and looked around, wondering what he was going to have me put on instead. I didn't see any other clothes around, but I figured professional photographers like him probably had special closets where they kept their props and models' clothes.

Suddenly Mr. Stanski was taking more pictures, before I even had a chance to ask him where he kept the extra clothes. "Um, Mr. Stanski," I said, "what clothes do you want me to put on?"

He gave me a strange look.

"Never mind about the clothes," he said. "I think that about wraps it up for today." He handed me the twenty dollars while I was putting my jeans back on. Then he asked, "Same time tomorrow, Garth?"

"I don't think so, Mr. Stanski," I said, "I didn't like taking off my clothes."

"Oh, come on, Garth, it's no big deal. What do you have to hide—I'm a guy, too. Besides, you'll *have* to come, Garth. If you don't, I'll show the police those pictures I took of you naked, and you'll be in big trouble with the law," he said. "You might even go to juvenile court for this."

Mr. Stanski had tricked me good. One thing my mother knew these days was the law. She hates the way so many guilty criminals walk the streets. If I broke the law, I know she'd make me go to jail. I was trapped— what else could I do but come back tomorrow?

"Okay, I'll be back," I mumbled.

"Don't worry, Garth, you're a special client. I'll make sure you don't get into trouble—of course, only as long as you do what I say. I'll tell you what—I'll pay you twenty-*five* dollars tomorrow." I used to think Mr. Stanski was an all-right guy, but now I wasn't so sure.

The next day Mr. Stanski had another man there with him. "Garth, this is Sam. Sam's a good friend of mine. I'm just going to take a few pictures of you and Sam having a little fun."

"What kind of fun?" I asked.

"Look, just remember who's in charge—me. If you do what I tell you to, nothing is going to happen to you. If not, well, Garth, I wouldn't try and find out if I were you," Mr. Stanski said.

"Look kid," said Sam, "you got nothing to worry about. We're just going to have a *good* time together."

Downstairs, Mr. Stanski told me to undress. Then Sam started undressing.

"Hey, kid," he said, "don't look so worried. I don't have anything you don't have."

Then Sam made me touch him and do all sorts of gross things to him. It was awful, but I was scared not to. How could I be so stupid, I kept thinking, to get into this mess? I never would have guessed Mr. Stanski was like this. He seemed so normal before. I had trusted him.

Mr. Stanski took pictures, saying how great it looked and what a good kid I was. It was the worst time in my whole life, and I wanted to puke. In fact, the second I got home I *did* puke.

When Mom came home, she took one look at me, felt my forehead and said, "Garth, are you sick?"

I didn't even answer.

"Why is your face so green?" she asked.

I thought about Sam and all the weird stuff he made me do. Then I couldn't help myself. I started crying and crying. I couldn't stop.

Mom sat on the bed and put her arm around me. "Want to talk about it, Garth?" she asked. How could I begin to tell her what had happened?

"Look, Garth," she said, "you're my son. Even though we have our disagreements, I care about you. When you *are* ready to talk, I'm ready to listen. I love you, Garth." She kissed my forehead.

That made me cry harder. When Dad came home he found us still sitting there, Mom hugging and me crying.

"What's all the commotion, gang?" he asked.

"Honey," Mom told Dad, "something *awful* must have happened to Garth. He hasn't cried so hard since his dog died."

Dad sat down on the bed on the other side of me, gently held my chin, and looked straight into my eyes.

"Son," he said, "what could possibly be so awful? Nothing could be bad enough that you can't tell your old man."

I told them everything.

You know, they didn't even get angry with me. They kept telling me over and over, "Garth, don't worry, we'll take care of you now. You didn't do *anything* wrong. It was Mr. Stanski and his friend—they did a terrible thing to you."

Together we reported to the police what happened. The police advised us to press charges so that Mr. Stanski and Sam would go to court. I was glad we did, because they admitted to doing this with lots of other kids just like me. Only those kids kept it a secret.

Watching Mr. Stanski and Sam get convicted and sentenced actually made me feel better even though being at the trial wasn't easy for me. Mom called my good feeling "a sense of justice."

I'm sorry I didn't get out of there when Mr. Stanski first told me to take off my clothes. And I'm sorry I fell for Mr. Stanski's blackmail about going to court for the nude pictures. The policeman said Mr. Stanski was guilty—he took the pictures. I was innocent.

I did get my dirt bike after all. Dad said I learned about "easy money" the hard way. Mom was on my side when I told the truth. I think she is going to make one nice lawyer.

Facts about Pornography

Garth willingly went into Mr. Stanski's house because he thought he had a job there. Instead, he became involved in child pornography. Garth didn't recognize the danger signals, such as Mr. Stanski's request to keep the modeling session secret. If he had, he could have avoided the situation. Garth, however, was not to blame. Mr. Stanski was an adult and used both his power and his control to get what he wanted from Garth.

What is pornography?

Pornography is a word used to describe any photographs, movies, or books made for the sole purpose of showing sexual activity. Child pornography describes pornography with children in it. Child pornography is illegal, but it still happens.

Children involved in pornography are frequently bribed into sexual contact with an adult or another child during the pornographic session.

How do adults get children involved in pornography?

Adults find children who want to earn money. Many children involved in pornography have run away from home and need money for food, shelter, or drugs.

What are the danger signals?

Danger signals are messages that tell you something may be wrong. Some common danger signals of any kind of sexual abuse are warnings like these:

"Don't tell anyone; this is our secret."

"If you tell anyone about this, no one will believe you."

"If you tell anyone, I will hurt you."

"If you tell anyone, you will get in big trouble."

"If you tell anyone, your parents won't love you anymore."

If you hear an adult make a statement like any of these, you should leave immediately and tell someone you trust about it.

If you are sexually abused by someone of the same sex, can you become homosexual?

Absolutely not! Homosexuality is a way of life that some people choose. Anyone who is forced into sexual activity with someone of the same sex is being abused, not making a choice.

After being sexually abused, it may be painful to talk about what happened, even with people you love and trust. Some victims feel the abuse is their fault because they overlooked the danger signals and allowed it to happen. But no victim needs to feel shame or guilt for sexual abuse—the abuser is always to blame for mistreating a child.

Sarah's Story

You Can't Judge a Book by Its Cover

Nanny has lived in the same house forever. "Don't you ever think about moving someplace new, Nanny?" I asked her once.

"Of course not, Sarah," she said. "This house is like an old friend to me. When I'm inside, I don't realize how much everything on the outside has changed. And believe me, after fifty-seven years, nothing's the same."

I think the real reason she doesn't move is that she'd have too much to pack. Nanny's house has fourteen rooms in it, and every one is filled. She saves everything—Daddy's old toys, dresses from the last forty years, and even every Sears catalog she ever got.

Before Nanny retired, she was a librarian. Her house has so many books in it that she could start her own library if she wanted. The book shelves are stuffed with books, and there are stacks of books on every table, especially in the living room. "Books are cookies for the mind," Nanny says. "You can live without them, but they sweeten your brain with thought."

26

Nanny also likes real cookies. Every Saturday morning is filled with both books and cookies. Nanny reads in her big stuffed armchair while I curl up with a book on the sofa. Proust, Nanny's favorite French author, said that certain smells and tastes bring back memories. To remember our special Saturday mornings, Nanny makes chocolate chip cookies. She waits until I come over to bake them. That way we can smell them in the oven. As soon as I smell those cookies, I drop my book and run into the kitchen to eat them hot out of the oven.

One Saturday morning, though, Nanny had run out of chocolate chips. It's hard to believe Nanny could run out of anything, especially chocolate chips, considering how she feels about chocolate. "People who love chocolate are sweeter," Nanny always says.

"But our mailman is always eating chocolate bars," I said, "and he's a grouch."

"Think how grouchy he'd be if he *didn't* eat chocolate."

27

Nanny said. Nanny finds a way to make everything look good. When she slipped on the ice and broke her hip last year, she figured it was good because she didn't break her back.

"Nanny, we don't have to have chocolate chip cookies," I told her.

"But we do, Sarah," Nanny said, shaking her head. "It would be bad luck not to."

I wasn't surprised Nanny had to have chocolate chips. She can be quite stubborn, especially about luck. Nanny is smart after reading so much, but she is also superstitious. She always makes me leave her house from the same door I entered. When I spill salt, she makes me throw some of it over my left shoulder and make a wish. And I'm positive the arthritis in her hands is from knocking on wood so often.

"I'll walk to the corner store and get some chocolate chips," I said.

"And I'll come with you," Nanny said, walking toward the coat closet.

The sidewalks were way too icy for Nanny to walk safely. "You stay here," I told her. "I'll be back before you can finish the next chapter of your book."

I took *Swiss Family Robinson* with me to read while I walked to the store.

When I was little I used to believe in the superstition, "Step on a crack and break your mother's back." It was easy to jump the cracks in the sidewalk around my house because the sidewalks are new. But on Nanny's street the sidewalks are old and full of cracks. The tree roots grew so large that they pushed the sidewalk into mounds, making it hard to jump over the cracks. These days I usually don't worry about cracks, but I guess I'm still a little superstitious. I still jump over the crack made by the big oak tree in front of the McFarley mansion.

As cracks go, it's big. When we first noticed what a big crack it was, Nanny and I made up a story about falling into it and landing in China. By now I'm so used to jumping over the McFarley crack that I consider it bad luck not to.

As I was walking and reading, I got to the exciting part where the pirates attack the Robinson family at the same time I got to the McFarley crack. I forgot to jump over it and tripped instead. I fell and my book went flying over the ice. A man saw me fall. He picked up my book for me and helped me to my feet.

"Are you okay?" the man asked.

"Yes, sir," I replied, brushing the snow off my pants. "Thanks for helping me." I knew I had never seen him before because of his ears. They were big and stuck out far. Even someone who doesn't usually look at ears would notice them.

On my way back from the store, I saw the same man sitting in his car. I walked past him, remembering to jump over the crack this time.

"That looked like a good book you were reading," he called out the window.

"It is," I said.

"Want to see what I'm reading?" he asked.

I walked over to his car and looked in the window.

"Look here," the man said, pointing to his pants.

I was so surprised I dropped my book and the bag of chocolate chips. Something was sticking out of his pants, and it was bigger and straighter than his ears.

I ran back to Nanny's as fast as I could.

When I told her what happened, she called the police. While we were waiting for them to come, I couldn't help thinking about the McFarley crack. When I forgot to jump over it, I tripped and fell. When I jumped over it, that man did something bad to me. It looked like bad luck either way. Since no one knew about luck more than Nanny, I asked her about it.

"That's life in a cookie jar — crumby sometimes," she said. "Luck is one way of looking at things that we can't explain in any other way. You can only talk about luck after you get over the fright or pain of whatever happened. Then it's usually easy to see that it could have been worse."

Nanny could probably imagine lots of worse things that might have happened to me on my walk, but I can't think of any.

Facts about Exhibitionism

Very few people go through life without encountering a situation such as Sarah's. Exhibitionism, or showing one's private parts in public, is probably the most common sexual abuse that occurs. One reason exhibitionism is shocking is that most children have never seen an erect penis on an adult. They wonder if what they see is really possible.

What is exhibitionism?

Exhibitionism is exposing the penis, usually erect, in order to shock or frighten someone else. Some exhibitionists also expose their buttocks. If exhibitionists are women, they expose their breasts for the same purpose.

Why do people expose themselves?

Seeing the shocked or frightened look on another person's face gives the exhibitionist pleasure. Most exhibitionists are shy, meek, and immature people.

Are exhibitionists dangerous?

Most of the time, exhibitionists are not dangerous. Exposing oneself in public, however, is not normal and may lead to more dangerous behavior. Even if you feel embarrassed about it, you should tell someone if this happens to you. Whenever you report an exhibitionist, you do yourself and those around you a favor. If the police can catch the exhibitionist, he or she may be able to get counseling.

Daddy's Little Girl

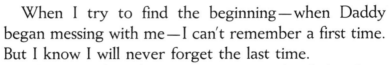

When I try to find the beginning—when Daddy began messing with me—I can't remember a first time. But I know I will never forget the last time.

I do remember the exact moment I decided to be a figure skater. Daddy took me and my sister Katie to the Great Ice Show. We sat in the front row. "Only the best for my little Jenny" was what Daddy said. The coliseum darkened. Then a single spotlight appeared on Julie Springer, the show's star. She wore the most beautiful costume I'd ever seen. Julie skated to the music, a popular love song, and her skates barely touched the ice. I tingled with excitement watching her.

At the end, the audience stood and applauded. Some people threw roses at her feet. She picked up the flowers and waved to the audience. Then she turned and smiled directly at me. There was Julie Springer standing alone on the ice—the center of attention. That was the moment I knew I wanted to skate.

That night, while we were all getting dressed to go to

the show, I overheard Daddy and Mummy fighting in their bedroom. They fight all the time.

"You look fat in that blue dress. Don't you have anything else to wear?" Daddy said to Mummy.

"Tom, why can't you stop picking on me? You married a person, not a mannequin," she said.

"Jacqueline, I married a *thin* person. You're so fat I'm embarrassed to be seen with you anymore," he said.

"Then don't," she shouted. "Go without me! You always look perfect on the outside, Tom, but inside you're nothing but hot air!"

Daddy stormed out of the room, slamming the door behind him. He marched downstairs to the liquor cabinet and poured himself a drink. Daddy has a horrible temper, and it's scary when he loses it. Lots of times when he's angry, he breaks things like dishes or glasses.

Sometimes when he gets mad, Daddy leaves the house and doesn't come back for hours. After he and Mummy fight, they go for days without talking to each other.

This time, Katie ran into my room. She was crying.

"Do you think we'll miss the show now, Jenny?" she asked.

"Of course not. You know Daddy keeps his word," I told her.

I never talk much around Daddy but Katie doesn't know how to be quiet. Sometimes she talks so much that Daddy yells, "Katie, shut up before you drive me crazy!"

Then Katie starts to cry and runs to Mummy, telling her what an awful daddy he is.

Daddy usually tells Katie she should be more like me. "Jenny knows how to be a good girl," he says. "Why can't you ever act like her?"

Then Mummy says to Katie, "Sweetheart, it's not worth trying to be like Jenny. Daddy will *never* think anyone is as good as Jenny."

I don't think Mummy should say that. Mummy doesn't have a scary temper like Daddy but she says things to hurt my feelings. If I tell her someone picked on me, she says, "Well, what did you do to get her angry, Jenny?" It seems like she never really sticks up for me or takes my side. So I usually don't tell her things. When I'm at home, I don't talk much to anyone.

The night of the Great Ice Show, Mummy stayed home, just like she said she would. Daddy had paid a lot of money for the front row seats and he was angry that she didn't come with us. He didn't talk on the way to the show. But I knew he'd be okay once we got there. He's different in public than he is at home. In front of other people he's *always* nice.

People tell Daddy how great he looks for his age. He should look great—he spends enough time working on it. He jogs every day and has run in twelve marathons. He likes all sports—"anything to sweat," Mummy says.

Ever since I can remember, Daddy has encouraged me to be athletic. He taught me to swim and play tennis, baseball, and basketball. He even showed me how to lift weights.

"Jenny, don't ever let yourself go like your mother has," Daddy always says. "Your mother used to have a great figure. She looked terrific. But now she's so out of shape I don't see how she can stand looking at herself."

How a person's body looks is pretty important to Daddy. Whenever he takes a shower, he walks down the hall past my room, naked, with his towel wrapped around his neck. And he knows we will all see him, because it's a rule in our house that Katie and I have to keep our bedroom doors open.

When I was little Daddy let me take showers with him. He'd soap me up all over. I liked it when he washed my back—he always tickled it. Then it would be my turn to soap him. "It's only fair, Jenny," he'd tell me. "And don't forget to soap *everything*." As I got older, I didn't like doing that, so I made up reasons I couldn't take a shower with him. He never really forced me, but let Katie shower with him instead.

Daddy always says I'm the only person in the world

who understands him. That's because I don't fight with him. But I don't understand him at all. I just know how to get along with him and how to keep out of his way when he's in a bad mood.

After the Great Ice Show, I asked Daddy if I could take figure skating lessons.

"Of course, honey," he said. "You know I like to see you try new sports."

Before the first lesson, Daddy took me shopping. First he bought me a fancy skating outfit. Then he asked to see the most expensive pair of skates in the store. The salesman said, "Sir, don't you think you should wait to see if your daughter likes ice skating before investing so much on equipment?"

"Oh, you don't know my little Jenny," Daddy told the man, putting his arm around me. "She's a natural athlete, just like her father."

Daddy was right. I felt I was born to skate. After a few months of lessons, the coach told Daddy, "Jenny has the natural talent to be a star if she puts her mind to it. But frankly, figure skating requires an enormous sacrifice."

"What kind of sacrifice, Coach?" Daddy asked.

"For one thing, it's expensive. And Jenny will have to give more time to practice than she could ever imagine," the coach said.

"Well, I'm willing to meet the financial part," Daddy said, turning to me. "Jenny, are you willing to put in all the work? Is skating what you *really* want?"

"Yes, Daddy, it is. I know I can do it, too," I told him.

I also knew it was what Daddy wanted for me.

As soon as I began entering the skating tournaments, I began winning. Coach was right about the work. It was more sacrifice than I'd ever imagined. I skated at least four to five hours a day—two hours in the morning before school even began. In addition to skating, I took ballet lessons three times a week. By the time I hit the bed at night I was exhausted and fell asleep quickly.

Poor Mummy and Daddy were stuck with the bills. The private lessons, the ice-time, the customized skates, the costumes, and the travel expenses really added up. To help pay for everything, Mummy took a part-time job as a salesperson at the mall several nights a week.

It was after Mummy began working that Daddy started coming into my room at night. He'd lie down beside me, hugging and kissing me gently. Even though he could be in a bad mood at times, I loved him. I liked it when he hugged me at night—it made me feel close to him. I always pretended to be asleep and it was kind of like a nice dream.

After a while, he began to climb under the covers with me. He'd pull up my nightie and rub his body against me. Daddy didn't come into my room every night. He only did it on the nights Mummy was working, once or twice a week.

Soon Daddy started putting his hand between my legs touching me everywhere. Did *all* fathers do this stuff? I had no one to ask. I didn't like it, and I felt trapped and ashamed of myself. It was probably all my fault for liking the cuddling at first and for always pretending to be asleep. Maybe if Daddy knew I was awake, he would have stopped. After all, he never talked about it. At breakfast he always acted like nothing had ever happened.

The state championships were coming up soon. If I placed first I could get a big-name coach and have a chance in the national competition. But I had to do my best—only my best could win me the title. I didn't want anything or anyone to interfere, and that included Daddy.

Whenever Daddy left my room at night, I had trouble sleeping. I'd lie awake for hours, sometimes even until daylight. The next day I was always tired and would make a lot of mistakes at practice. Each time Coach asked me what was wrong, I'd say I was just having a bad day.

"Everyone has days like that, Jenny," Coach would tell me. "The athletes who make it to the top are the ones that stick with it through those bad days."

If I could just get Daddy to leave me alone, I thought, I wouldn't have so many bad days. Then I had an idea. That week, I wore two pairs of underpants, leotards, and a pair of sweatpants to bed every night. If Daddy was going to touch me, he'd have to wake me up. I didn't think he would, since all this time he had pretended that nothing was happening.

Two nights later Daddy came into my room, crawled under the covers, and lifted my nightgown. My heart was pounding so hard I was afraid he would hear it. I clenched my teeth as tight as I could to keep still and pretended as usual to be asleep. I was worried about what Daddy would do next.

When he felt my sweatpants, Daddy jumped out of my bed, slammed the door, and ran downstairs. I heard him pour himself a drink. Then he smashed more dishes and glasses than I had ever heard him break before. Finally it was over. Daddy went to bed before Mummy came home.

We were all so used to ignoring Daddy's temper tantrums, especially Mummy and I, that none of us mentioned the broken dishes the next morning. Mummy didn't even ask him what was wrong. At breakfast, I didn't talk and tried to think about skating instead.

I always get butterflies before I skate in a competition. The state championships were no exception. But as soon as the music started and I began to concentrate on skating, the butterflies disappeared. In fact, I felt like a butterfly myself—gliding on the ice, the skirt from my costume fluttering in the wind I was creating with my own movements.

When I finished my program, I took a deep bow and listened to the audience clap and cheer. Looking down at the ice, I saw flowers at my feet. I picked them up and looked at the audience, wondering who had thrown them. For that moment the world felt all mine. It was just as I had dreamed it would be, only better, and it was worth all the sacrifice it had taken to get it. Inside I felt like I could do anything I tried.

I came in second. I was disappointed, but Coach reminded me that I'm still young. "Keep up the good work," he said, "because next year you have an even better chance."

Daddy has never come into my room again, and I wish I had tried to stop him sooner. I'm still afraid at night when I hear him come upstairs. Maybe someday I'll be able to tell someone about it. Then I'll find out if all fathers do that.

Facts about Incest

Jenny stopped her father's sexual contact with her. The danger is that he, like most adults guilty of incest, will begin doing it again unless Jenny tells someone about it.

What is incest?

Incest is sexual contact between a child and an adult who belong to the same family. Incest is harmful to the child, and it is also against the law.

Who commits incest?

Much, but not all, incest occurs between fathers and daughters. Other adults, like stepfathers, grandfathers, uncles, brothers-in-law, and mothers, also commit incest.

Most fathers, of course, have close, loving relationships with their daughters without having sexual contact. Fathers who abuse their daughters often don't realize the harm they are doing to them. They may look at their daughters like property, believing they have the right to do whatever they want. There is absolutely *no* excuse, however, for incest.

Can incest be avoided?

Of all the types of sexual abuse, incest is probably the most difficult to avoid. Children love and trust their parents, and it is hard for them to believe that a parent would do anything to harm them. Sometimes the extra attention and physical closeness during incest feel good. But unlike incest, healthy affection is never a secret and is never forced on anyone.

Why does incest happen?

Adults seeking sexual contact with children are very immature. They look to a child for the closeness they should seek in adult relationships. They choose children who they think will trust and obey them, and who will keep the sexual contact a secret.

Incest is the whole family's problem.

Incest affects all members of the family. Mothers are often unaware that incest is going on because it is kept so secret. Even if a mother notices changes in her family, she may not realize that those changes are caused by incest. Some mothers *do* know, but they are afraid to act. A mother in this situation fears that if she confronts the father with the abuse, he will hurt her and hurt the child even more. And some mothers just don't *want* to know. They already have more problems than they can handle, so they pretend the incest doesn't exist.

Whose fault is incest?

Incest is the fault of the adult involved. It is not the child's fault. And, unless she is committing incest herself, a mother is not to blame for the incest that goes on in her family. If she doesn't know about it, she cannot be expected to stop it. If she *does* know about it and does nothing to stop it, she is very much at fault. But when someone she loves and trusts commits incest against her child, a mother may have trouble believing and accepting it. She may need some time to understand what has happened.

How can you stop incest?

Until incest is reported, both the abuser and the victim have serious problems. Any adult who has sexual contact with a child needs counseling. The victim, too, needs professional counseling to get over his or her confusion and feelings of guilt and shame.

Sometimes an abuser is committing incest with two or more children in a family. He or she will tell each child, "If you do what I want, I won't touch your sister." Victims can never know if that is true. The best way to protect all family members is not to keep incest a secret.

You want to trust that people are good and won't hurt you, especially your own family. But if anyone uses that trust to hurt you, you should tell someone about it.

If you can't tell a member of your family, or if the family member you have told doesn't believe you, tell someone outside your family. Incest isn't your fault, and it doesn't have to continue.

Don't Call Me, I'll Call You

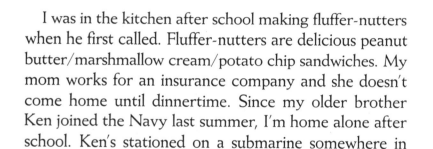

I was in the kitchen after school making fluffer-nutters when he first called. Fluffer-nutters are delicious peanut butter/marshmallow cream/potato chip sandwiches. My mom works for an insurance company and she doesn't come home until dinnertime. Since my older brother Ken joined the Navy last summer, I'm home alone after school. Ken's stationed on a submarine somewhere in the middle of the ocean. He used to take me to McDonald's after school and we'd eat Big Macs. Now I fend for myself.

The telephone rang. I answered it.

"Hello, McNeill's," I said.

I couldn't hear anyone on the other end.

"Hello, McNeill's," I repeated, this time shouting a little in case it was a bad connection.

Still no answer. Maybe it was a wrong number.

"What number did you want?" I asked.

"What number is this?" asked a voice on the other end. He sounded like one of my brother's friends.

"This is 344-8722," I replied. "Is that the number you wanted?"

But I heard the receiver click—he had hung up. Some people are in such a hurry they forget to be nice, I thought.

I finished making two fluffer-nutters and carried them into the family room to play video games while I ate. Afterwards I was going to play street hockey with my friends Greg and Paul. We're practicing hard in case street hockey ever becomes an Olympic sport. We want to be the first Olympic street hockey gold medalists.

Just as I was zipping up my jacket, the telephone rang.

"Hello, McNeill's," I said.

No answer on the other end. Darn it. I was hoping it wasn't that wrong number again because I had to get out to play. Greg and Paul were tapping on my window, waving for me to come out.

"Hello, who is this, and who do you want?" I asked.

"Is your mother there?" whispered the voice on the other end. I could barely hear him. It was that guy again.

"No, my mom's not here right now. Can I take a message and have her call you when she gets home?"

"Tell me something," the guy asked, "do you wear your mother's pantyhose when she isn't looking?"

Now that was a really *weird* question. I didn't like this mystery caller.

"Listen buddy," I said, "that's a dumb question. Of course I don't!"

"Then you should," he said, and hung up the phone again.

Greg and Paul were pounding on the window by now, so I ran outside.

They were busy talking about the Olympics and how we were going to get gold medals and be on the cover of *Sports Illustrated*. I scored ten goals, and by the time we finished playing hockey, I sort of forgot about the weird phone call.

At dinner, Mom asked me how my day had been.

"It was okay," I said. "I got a perfect score on my math test, Buddy gave me a double of his favorite sticker, and I scored ten hockey goals. By the way, Mom," I asked, "did you ever get a weird phone call?"

"What do you mean, John?"

"Oh, just weird, you know, someone asking something stupid?"

"John, did you get a harassing phone call?"

"What's 'harassing' mean?"

"That's when someone calls to bother or to scare you."

Well, mystery man asked me a dumb question, but it didn't scare me. I mean, that guy asked if I wore *pantyhose*. How could I talk about that with my mother? She might think maybe there was something weird about me!

"No, Mom, I just heard about it somewhere."

That night the phone rang. I was relieved when my mom answered it, hoping maybe it would be mystery man. Then she could tell him not to call back. But it was Aunt Beth, one of Mom's sisters, and they spent an hour making plans for a party for their other sister, Janet, who is having a baby next month. Next Mom called her friend Barbara, and they talked all the way through my favorite TV show. Then it was time for me to go to bed. Even if mystery man had tried to call, he didn't stand a chance of getting through.

The next day, about the same time, just as I was adding the potato chips to my fluffer-nutter, the phone rang. I was expecting Paul to call and tell me to bring my extra hockey stick. He broke his and is waiting to get a new one for his birthday next week.

"Hello, McNeill's," I said.

"I saw your mother's black lace bra, and I think you should try it on," said a voice. It was the same voice that called yesterday.

"Listen," I said, "I told you before. You ask dumb questions and I want you to stop calling me. Who are you anyway?" But he just hung up on me again. The jerk, I thought.

My palms were sweaty now, and I could feel my heart pounding. What kind of a guy gets his kicks out of asking a kid about his mother's underwear? I was getting worried and hoped he'd never call again.

He didn't call the next two days. I figured it was because it was the weekend. On Monday, as soon as I got home from school, even though I was hungry, I went straight outside to play. I didn't want to be home for mystery man to bother me.

The next day it rained so we couldn't play outside. I wanted to go to Paul's house, but both our mothers work and neither of us is allowed to have friends over when they are gone. So, like it or not, I had to stay home alone.

I decided to trick mystery man. I took the phone off the hook during the time he usually called. But as soon as I put the receiver back, the phone rang, and sure enough it was him.

"Hey, McNeill," he said in that voice I was really beginning to hate, "I see you standing there. Pull down your pants for me so I can look at you. You better do it or you'll be sorry."

I looked out the window. The rain was coming down in buckets, and the street was deserted. Outside the window I could see the row of apartment buildings on the other side of the street. Mystery man could be looking out of any one of those windows. What if he had a gun pointed at me? I would die of embarrassment if anyone saw me pull down my pants but I didn't think I had much choice. Anything was better than getting shot. I quickly pulled my pants down and up again—mystery man could look but he wasn't going to get a *long* look.

"There, I did it," I told him. "And don't ask me to do it again."

"Thanks, McNeill," he said and hung up before I had a chance to say anything more to him.

I walked over to the window. My legs were shaking, and I felt like crying. I pulled down the shade, checked the door lock, and then sat down to figure out what to do next. I was scared. And even though I had taken a shower two days in a row, I still felt dirty.

What if mystery man came to my house? If he could see me then he must know where I live. And worse yet, what if he came to my house when Greg and Paul were knocking on the window like they do every afternoon when the weather is nice? It wasn't going to be easy, but I had to tell my mom.

I looked at the clock on the wall—it was close to six. Mom would be home any minute if she didn't get caught in rush-hour traffic. After what seemed liked forever, I finally heard her key opening the back door.

"Hi, John," she said. I was so happy to hear her voice, so glad to see someone I could trust.

"Hi, Mom," I replied.

"John," she asked, "I tried calling you earlier to remind you to put the chicken in the oven, but the phone was busy for over an hour. Who on earth could you possibly have been talking to for so long?"

Before she could take off her coat, I was telling her the whole story from the first call to the last. When I finished, she hugged me and told me that lots of people get calls like that. This time she called them obscene phone calls. Together we reported mystery man to the police.

The police were great. They told me they get reports on obscene callers all the time. In fact, at least a half dozen people in our precinct had called that week to report a man asking about women's underwear. Like me, a few other people had also believed his threats and had obeyed his commands.

The police said they would ask the phone company to put a tracing device on our phone. If mystery man called again, maybe they could catch him.

The next morning, Mom asked if I wanted her to come home early from work to be with me when mystery man called. Now that I wasn't afraid anymore, I told her she didn't have to.

That afternoon, just as I was finishing the fluffernutters, the phone rang. I couldn't wait to trap mystery man forever on tape.

"Hi there," I said in a friendly voice, "what do you want today?"

I think mystery man was a little surprised to hear me so pleasant because he took a minute or so to answer. Meanwhile my hands were getting sweaty on the receiver. I wanted to make sure the device had time to trace him. I repeated, "Hi, what do you want today?"

"McNeill," he finally said, "you look good today. Listen, I want you to take off your pants and put on your mother's laciest underpanties."

I wasn't scared anymore. I knew there was *no* way for him to see me because all the shades in the entire house were down.

"Okay, but you'll have to wait a minute—I have to find the laciest," I told him. I figured five minutes should be long enough to make him wait.

"All right, I have them on, but they're a little tight."

"Thanks, McNeill, thanks, you look real good, real good."

The police traced the call to a man who lived across the city from us. He was unemployed and feeling sorry for himself. So he spent all day looking for suckers like me. But I'm not a sucker anymore and won't ever be one again.

Now I never give out my name when I answer the phone, and I never let on that I'm home alone. Just to be sure, I've also stopped making fluffer-nutters. They remind me too much of mystery man.

Facts about Obscene Phone Calls

Not every obscene caller will make the same demands that John's mystery man did. Most callers probably wouldn't ask you to do anything. They usually just want to shock you. Practically everyone with a telephone gets a call like this sometime in his or her life. The following information will help you know what to do if it happens to you.

What is an obscene phone call?

The word "obscene" means repulsive or disgusting. Most people think of obscene words as "dirty words." In fact, you've probably heard some of these words. But it's still a shock when someone calls just to say them to you. Some callers won't talk but will instead make heavy breathing sounds into the phone.

A harassing phone call is one made to scare you or bother you. Instead of using obscene language, the caller will try to frighten you in another way.

Who makes obscene phone calls?

Most people who make obscene calls are lonely or having some sort of problem in life. Some are unemployed, while others might be mentally ill or having trouble with their families. They know they can shock others with dirty language, and they make these calls to feel important. Bothering someone who can't see them gives them a feeling of power. Most of the people who make these phone calls would probably be afraid to say the same things to someone in person.

What should you do if you get an obscene call?

As soon as you realize that it is an obscene phone call, hang up immediately. Don't ever continue to listen to the caller. Tell an adult in your house and report the call to the police.

Can you prevent obscene phone calls?

Unless you never answer your phone, you can't prevent an obscene phone call. Anyone can dial random numbers and reach yours, even if it is not listed in the telephone directory. You can, however, discourage someone from calling back a second time. The following rules will help:

1. Always answer the phone by saying "hello." *Never* give your name. The person calling should always identify him or herself, but *you* don't have to.

2. If you suspect someone has gotten a wrong number, ask the caller what number he or she wanted. Then tell the person if it is wrong. Never give out your number!

3. If someone is obscene on the phone, hang up.

4. *Always* report the phone call to your police department, even if it is just one call. If the obscene calls continue, the police will advise the telephone company to use a tracing device to track down the caller.

5. *Never* let a caller know you are home alone. If someone asks to speak to either your mother or your father when you are home alone, say "She (or he) is busy right now and will have to call you back. May I take a message?" If the caller doesn't want to leave a name and number, he or she will probably try to reach your parents again another time.

Marti's Story

The Susan B. Anthony Report

After having five sons, Joyce and Philip (that's what I call my parents) were so sure I'd be a boy that they picked the name Martin for me before I was even born. It was the name of the main character in the novel Philip was writing at the time. When they found out I was a girl, they were too excited to think of another name. Joyce suggested shortening Martin to Marti and Philip loved the idea. It was the first time, and probably the last, that they agreed on anything.

Until I ate at my friend Kristen's house, I thought that all families argued at dinner. These days the fighting usually starts when Joyce mentions something she heard on a talk show. She teaches a course on the effect television has on women's issues. Then Philip disagrees with her, and they start arguing. Soon everyone else at the table is taking sides. We all shout so loudly I wonder if any of us really listens to what the others say. After dinner, Philip and Joyce usually walk around the neighborhood continuing their dinner argument while

the rest of us clean up. That's when the real fighting begins.

"I'm not washing the dishes tonight. I did it two nights ago," Matt shouts at Peter. Peter's in charge because he's the oldest.

"You never want to wash, Matt," Peter yells. He's right. Matt tries to do the easy stuff, like clear the table, instead. Joe will do anything to get out of doing his chores, like paying Jimmy to do them for him. Jimmy buys so many tapes that he's glad to earn the money. Mostly, the older boys settle the issue of who does what out on the porch where they wrestle each other. Once Jimmy broke Peter's nose and still wanted him to do the dishes. "He lost, didn't he?" Jimmy said.

I don't fight much with Peter, Matt, or Joe because they spend so much time fighting each other. I fight with Jimmy enough, but it's Chuck, the brother next to me, who really knows how to get my goat.

The night Philip's play, "Wise Soul," previewed at the

university theater where Joyce is teaching, we all went to a fancy restaurant for dinner. Chuck sat across the table from me.

"Stop looking at me that way," I told Chuck.

"What way?" he asked. "I'm just looking at you."

"Joyce, will you please tell Chuck not to look at me that way?" I asked my mother.

"Marti, can't your brother look at you?" she said. I should have asked Philip instead. Joyce always answers a question by asking another question. I decided not to bug Philip, who was too nervous about the performance of his play to take my side effectively.

I just had to tackle Chuck myself. The best way to get back at Chuck was to copy everything he did. That always drives him crazy. So whenever Chuck lifted his fork, I'd lift mine. If he scratched his nose, I'd scratch mine.

"Stop it, Marti," Chuck said, "or I'll beat your face in."

"Try it," I told him, smiling, knowing he couldn't do it in the restaurant, since he was between Joe and Matt who'd beat *his* face up, because they always take my side against Chuck and Jimmy.

When Chuck threw his milk at me, Joyce and Philip were so mad at him they made him stay in his room for a week. It was one of my best victories.

Last year Joyce and Philip were worried that because I was the youngest in the family, I might not get enough responsibility.

"Marti, your mother and I want to get you a cat,"

Philip told me one day. "You'd take care of it all by yourself—feed it, clean the litter box, let it in and out of the house."

"It's a good idea," I told him, "but I'd rather have a lion. I read about a woman who had a lion in her home. Philip, just think, with a lion I'd become responsible enough to run for president of the United States someday."

"Out of the question," he said.

"The lion or president?" I asked.

"The lion. I expect you to be president," he said. "And if you're really smart, you'll appoint your mother secretary of defense. No one can win against her."

The next week Philip and Joyce arrived home with the most adorable kitten I've ever seen. He had long, fluffy white fur and blue eyes. I named him Anthony after Susan B. Anthony, the champion of women's rights. If Anthony was going to be a member of the Selby family, he'd have to be able to defend himself.

As usual, Joyce and Philip were right. Having a cat turned out to be a big responsibility, all mine. And I'm not sure Anthony liked his name, because one day he chewed up my book report on Susan B. Anthony.

I didn't find out until the morning it was due. Joyce had already left to teach a class, so I asked Philip for his advice.

"Marti, when you know a topic as well as you know about Susan B. Anthony, you should be able to rewrite it in no time at all," he said.

Then Philip fed Anthony for me and even made my

breakfast so I'd have extra time to finish the report. I guess since Philip's a writer he could relate to the pressure of a deadline.

Chuck and I walk to school together. The others take the school bus to the junior high and high school.

"I'm leaving without you if you don't come now," Chuck warned me. "I'm not going to get a detention because of you."

"Go without me," I said. "I can take care of myself."

When I finished the report I looked up at the clock. The bell would ring in only seven minutes and it takes me fifteen to get to school. I figured that if I ran fast and cut through the Oxmoor Apartments courtyard, I could make it on time.

The Oxmoor Apartments have been vacant and boarded up for over a year. Joyce is always calling City Hall to get them to do something about it, but nothing ever gets done. Although we're not allowed to go there, the older boys do anyway. Matt told me he caught Joe and Peter smoking cigarettes there. When he caught them, he made them do his chores for a week. If they didn't, he threatened to tell our mother. She would have had fits, being an ex-smoker who can't stand cigarettes.

I grabbed my York School jacket with my name on the back and ran out the door. Just as I was running through the courtyard, I heard someone yell, "Marti, wait a minute."

I turned around to see who was calling me. Before I knew what was happening, a man grabbed my arm and said, "I have a knife so follow me and I won't hurt you."

I looked straight at his face, giving him the look I give my brothers before I hit them—I call it my evil eye. Knife or no knife, I figured this couldn't be worse than fighting Jimmy. He's the dirtiest fighter I know.

I was scared. But more than anything, I was angry. After working so hard on that report, no one was going to make me late for school, not even a man who said he had a knife.

I yelled, "Let go of me, you creep!" Then I landed a swift kick on the man's knee, and clenched my fists and hit him on the nose as hard as I could. Soon I didn't care about my report anymore—I just wanted to get out of there alive. When I poked my finger in the man's eye, he let go of my arm. Then I ran out of there as fast as I could, screaming, "Fire, fire." I hoped someone would help me, but nobody did. That didn't surprise me, because no one is ever around there. When I got to school, I told my teacher what happened and begged her not to give me a detention for being late.

My teacher told the principal, who called the police. By the time they went over to the courtyard to look for the man, he was gone. I should have told them to look for my book report while they were there, but I was so upset I forgot.

That night at dinner, my brothers argued about who was going to find the guy and beat him up. "No one is going to look for that man, not even Philip," said Joyce. "He's too dangerous."

Because it had been such a traumatic day for me, Joyce and Philip let me join them on their evening walk.

We left the boys to fight about who would get stuck with my chores.

A week later the police called me. They were holding a suspect charged with raping an eight-year-old girl in an abandoned building a couple of blocks away. Sure enough, it was the same man who tried to attack me. With dark curly hair and a dimple in his chin, he was easy to identify. He was also wearing an eye patch over the eye I had poked with my finger.

My teacher didn't give me a detention for being late, but she did make me rewrite my book report—for the second time. I got an A on it. Philip said that was because I wrote it so many times. He told me that sometimes he has to write a chapter eighteen times. I couldn't imagine fifteen more things happening to my Susan B. Anthony book report.

Facts about Rape

Marti had a close brush with a rapist. The man who tried to rape her was looking for a victim. But Marti wasn't going to be anyone's victim. She knew she had to get away. Because the man was holding her, she fought to make him let go. Marti was lucky. Although it is impossible to prevent every rape, the following information can help you avoid getting raped. It will also help you if you have been raped.

What is rape?

Rape is *forced sexual contact* by another person.

Who rapes?

Most rapists are men. Usually, something very bad happened to them that made them mad at the world. They never learned to express that anger in a healthy way.

Many rapists are grownups who were sexually abused when they were children. They never got help, and they grew up feeling angry and powerless. Rapists think that hurting someone else will make them feel better.

You can't tell a rapist by looking at him or her. On the outside rapists are like everyone else. It is only on the inside that they are different.

Who gets raped?

Anyone can be the victim of rape—young or old, male or female, tall or short, fat or thin.

Most rapists, however, want to rape someone who appears weaker than they are. They look for an easy target, someone who looks unlikely to put up a fuss or protest.

How can you avoid getting raped?

Don't be an easy target.

Rapists look for someone who appears weak, so *look strong.* Stand straight and walk as if you know where you are going, even when you don't. If you look like the kind of person who will fight back, a rapist will probably stay away from you.

Use the buddy system.

Rapists look for children who are alone. Walk to school, wait for the bus, play, or run an errand with a buddy, or friend, whenever possible.

Don't wear clothes that give your name.

Personalized jackets and T-shirts are fun to have and to wear. It's all right to wear these things when you are at home, at someone's house, or with adults. But don't wear personalized clothing in public unless you know you will be with one of your parents all of the time.

Don't talk to strangers.

Rapists test their victims. They look for someone who pays attention to them or listens to them. They think that someone who talks to them will be less likely to put up a fight. They test their victim by asking questions like these:

> "What time is it?"
> "I'm lost. Can you give me some directions?"
> "What's your name?"

If you talk to a rapist, he will think that you are a person he can control and that you will probably do what he wants you to do.

Who is a stranger?

There is no way to tell a nice stranger from a bad

one. To be safe, *don't talk to any stangers!* A stranger is someone you have never seen before and whose name you don't know. Unless you are absolutely sure you have met the person before, walk away from anyone who talks to you. *Run away* from anyone you think is dangerous. Nice strangers know that children aren't supposed to talk to them and will not feel insulted when you leave.

Don't listen to threats.

After a rapist chooses a target, he threatens his victim. He tries scaring or bullying the victim into doing what he asks.

"I have a gun (or knife), so do what I say."
"I know where you live, and if you don't do what I say, I will get you later."
"Do what I say, and I won't hurt you."

Some rapists will lie, saying they have a weapon when they actually don't have one. Others really do have a weapon. What should you do then?

Don't trust anyone with a gun or a knife.

Don't follow anyone who threatens you with a weapon. Instead, run away. Even if the person promises not to hurt you, don't believe him or her. Most rapists won't keep their word.

If you are being held, scream, kick, and make a fuss to attract attention. Someone may hear you and come to help. Your actions may also scare the person into leaving you alone. Even if someone has a gun or a knife, you still have a chance to get away.

Never get in a car with a stranger.

A rapist won't always use his gun or knife if you don't get in the car or follow him. Your chance for safety is better on the sidewalk than in the car. You are better off running away or screaming. Fight any way you can — bite, scratch, hit, and kick.

Never follow a stranger into a building, including your own house.

You are safer outside a building, where someone might come to help you, than inside. If someone does follow you into your house and you know that no one else is home, leave the house as soon as you can. Run away and tell someone.

Get angry.

Angry children are *not* the kind of victims a rapist looks for. Even if you can't run away — if, for example, the rapist has grabbed your arm — get angry. Turn your fear into anger and scream, bite, kick, and hit. Do anything you can think of to show him you feel strong. Many children have escaped by fighting back and trying to attract attention.

What should you do if you do get raped?

Sometimes rape happens, even when victims fight back. If this happens to you, tell someone right away! Keeping your rape a secret will only hurt you more. Always remember that everyone who survives a rape did something right.

Rape victims need help to overcome their hurt and fear. If you can't tell a parent or a teacher, then call a rape crisis center (the telephone operator can assist you). The person at the rape crisis center will listen to you, believe you, and help you.

If you were raped and have never told anyone about it, do it now! You will feel better when you have told, even if it is hard to talk about. It is never too late to tell someone you trust about any rape that happened to you, no matter how long ago. Being raped is a terrible experience. The sooner you talk about it, the faster you can begin to heal.

Feeling Strong

You have the right to feel safe and to feel good about yourself. These are your personal rights, and to defend them, you must feel strong. Feeling strong, as Marti showed in the last chapter, is more a matter of mind than of muscle. Everyone can learn to feel strong.

Sometimes being strong will mean speaking up for your rights. Other times you may have to fight, kick, and scream for help to defend yourself. And in some cases, being strong will mean having the courage to tell your problem to an adult.

As Garth learned, sexual abusers want to keep their actions a secret so they won't get caught. But sexual abuse should never be kept a secret. To stop sexual abuse from continuing, you must bring it out into the open. By telling someone, you can prevent abuse from happening again, either to you or to another person.

Few problems are so big that you can't tell your parents. If a problem is so bad that you feel you can't tell them, you should tell someone else. Some situations, like Jenny's, already involve a parent. If you are being sexually abused by one parent and can't tell the other one, you must tell someone outside your family.

There are many people besides your parents who

care about your safety. Some of these people are your teachers, neighbors, minister or rabbi, scout leader, coach, police officers, and doctor. Choose one person you trust and talk about your situation. If that person does not offer to help you, choose someone else to tell.

If you are afraid to tell someone you know, then call one of these toll-free numbers:

> 1-800-422-4453 National Child Abuse Hotline
> (1-800-4-A-CHILD)
> 1-800-421-0353 Parents Anonymous Hotline
> 1-800-621-4000 National Runaway Hotline

When you call these numbers, you don't even have to give your name if you don't want to. The people who answer these phones will find help for you no matter what. If you can't reach someone at these numbers, then dial 0 or 911 and say to the operator, "I'm being abused, and I need to reach someone who will help me."

Talking about what has happened may be hard, but *not* talking about it is worse. If you keep your feelings of fear, anger, hurt, and confusion inside, you are likely to feel very lonely. It may even change the way you act toward your friends. Talking about these feelings and what caused them will help you feel more self-confident again.

Child abuse is against the law and must be reported to the proper authorities. In most places, these authorities are either the police or a local child-protection agency. Abusers who are caught face one of several consequences. The punishment depends on such factors as the nature of the abuse, the lawyers handling the case, or how a case is tried in court. Not all cases get to court as Garth's did, however. Some abusers are put into counseling programs, while others pay fines or serve jail terms. And some abusers get off scot-free. Nothing is done to them or for them.

You can help make your world safer. Learn to be aware of danger signals, and have the courage to speak up and act on situations that make you feel uncomfortable. When something doesn't feel right, tell someone about it. You deserve to feel safe all of the time.

About the Authors

Susan Neiburg Terkel holds a degree in Child Development and Family Relationships from Cornell University. Ms. Terkel has written for newspapers, magazines, and poetry journals and is the author of *Yoga Is for Me*. She lives in Hudson, Ohio, with her husband and three children.

Janice Elizabeth Rench, a native of Boston, lives in Cleveland, Ohio, where she is the Executive Director of the Cleveland Rape Crisis Center. A rape survivor herself, Ms. Rench specializes in the counseling of adults who were sexually abused as children. She also lectures on the prevention of rape and sexual abuse of children.

COLLIER HEIGHTS

DISCARDED

DEC 0 2 1987

24 COLLIER HEIGHTS

R00142 41480

J362.7044

Terkel, Susan Neiburg.
    Feeling safe, feeling strong : how to
avoid sexual abuse and what to do if it
happens to you / Susan N. Terkel &
Janice E. Rench. -- Minneapolis :
Lerner Publications Co., c1984.
    68 p. : ill. ; 23 cm.
    Summary: Fictional vignettes depict
acts of child sexual abuse, such as
pornography, incest, rape, and obscene
phone calls; and information on
handling such situations is offered.
    ISBN 0-8225-0021-3 (reinforced bdg.)
    1. Child molesting--Juvenile
literature.   2. Child molesting--
Prevention--Juvenile literature.
I. Rench, Janice E.   II. Title

GA   05 OCT 87   10752873   GAPAxc   84-9664